SUPERSTORM SANDY

The Aftermath at the New Jersey Shore

BRONVILLE SCOTT

PAGE PUBLISHING, INC.
New York, NY

First originally published by Page Publishing, Inc. 2016

ISBN 978-1-68348-693-0 (Paperback)
ISBN 978-1-68348-694-7 (Digital)

Printed in the United States of America

Dedication

This publication is dedicated to my dad, Bronville Russell Scott Sr., because without him, there would be no me.

Acknowledgment

I would like to thank the Red Cross. Throughout the four or five months of cleaning and the repairs being made after Sandy, the Red Cross provided a variety of goods and services that will forever stand out for those who were on the front line.

LONG BEACH ISLAND

The Atlantic Ocean is on the other side of this
sand hill. Only the skyline can be seen.

Boardwalk dislodged from the pilings along the beach.
Pilings only part of the boardwalk remaining.

The sand from the ocean settles inland wipes away the
boardwalk. Judging how high the sand is compared to the pilings.

Photos show piling saved house from structural damage above the car port. Underneath did not fair as well (minimal damage).

Photo illustrates why pilings are considered an important part of the landscape at the shore, where houses are built close to bodies of water.

These photos illustrate that the boardwalk was destroyed and depicts how bare the beach looks.

Photos of the backyard showing what destruction took place,
as well as, the boardwalk having been uplifted from the pilings.

Stairway that leads to the beach no longer accessable.

Backyard view shows various types of destruction.
Boardwalk non-existant.

Photos are a view of the back of the house and
the remants from the destruction of sandy.

Damages were so extensive a lot of houses were declared unsafe. An official document was affixed to specific houses, occupants were evacuated. Placard affixes to front door.

Different View: Same structure, #4, declared
unsafe for human occupancy.

This empty lot is where the house to the left stood.
Sand removal and grateing being conducted.

Fire hydrant left leaning. Photo illustrates that a lot
of sand was blown around (normally fire hydrant
standing only the red painted area is visible)

The house to the far left was lifted off of its foundation, having been relocated leaning against the house of the neighbor. The only evidence remaining of what was are the reminiscence of pilings where the house resided. Mountain of sand, to the right of the house, illustrates how much wind volicity Sandy exhibited and what was left afterwards.

House to the right shown leaning against the house of their neighbor. Some of the neighbor's belongings sitting out front where a curb existed, curb no longer visible.

Inspite of Sandy both houses still standing
and not completely destroyed.

Same house, different angle.

Although this house was displaced off its foundation, complete
ruination did not occur. As serious as the destruction from Sandy
had been, a prank was not conceived as being contemptible. A
note was nailed to the house charging one dollar ($ 1.00) per
photo; the results of so many people arriving to see a "freak
of nature". As many as 40 or more people stopped to look
at Sandy's handy work (taking photos) in a single day.

House totally collapsed, entire structre crushed.

Deck gaveway, collapsed on top of the roof of the car.

Photos show structural damage. Side and rear of the house no longer attached. The house fell onto the automobile. Can actually see appliances and other items, standing outside, that are inside the house.

From the rear of the house, these photos show the complete right side, 1/2 of the house destroyed. The only thing distinguishabe is the television dish.

A close look at a lot of items destroyed
that were inside of the house.

Photos show the house toppled forward, crushing the front of the dwelling the rear of the house tilted in an awkward position. The front entryway not accessible.

House as well as the neighbors, where minimal damage sustained

Some damage exists. Foundation appears
to be lifted from the ground.

The roof dropped completely on top of the house. Unable to go inside to look around at any damage or view any of the furnishings. Lawnchairs, table, and umbrella remained intact.

Outside wall was separated from the dwelling, can actually go into the garage area of the house - a door is not necessary.

View of the back of the house where the
lawn furniture sat out front.

Closer look at damage and destruction
where roof fell on the garage area.

The front of the house was completely dislodged from
the structure. This depicts what was left of the living
room… the furnishings were completely gone.

Another angle shows what little amount of furnishings
were not destroyed or blown away as a result of
the storm. Again looking from outside.

Looking from the outside at the destruction inside.

Complete front wall of the house no longer attached
to the dwelling. Standing outside; what was left of
any furnishings, only a couch can be seen

Deck at the rear of the house was wrecked.

Household appliances being discarded.

Toys that were being thrown away.

Residents throwing away furniture,
appliances, as well as, personal items.

House being gutted. Inside walls removed, only the beams
are visible. Walls to be replaced with new sheet rock.

Damaged floors being removed, will be replaced.

Photos show house is totaled.

Rear of the house.

An interior look at Cramer's Paint and Hardware Store.
Water damage inside of the store causesd such destruction
that the store had to clear out all of its merchandise.

A multitude of cans of paint, tools, solvents, and
sundries were discarded (thrown away).

Shelves showing rust from water. All of
the shelving was thrown away.

The hanging boards were also discarded.

Cranmer's total clean out of everything

CRANMER'S
PAINT & HARD
220
TOOLS
SUNDRIES
SALE
VAN DYK
609-492-1511

Photos show that along the curb a row of appliances
and furnishings that are lining the street.

The items are being discarded, as depicted in the photos.

Sandy passes by this particular house. Hardly any destruction to the property, house included. Sustained some water damage to the interior—appliances were thrown away.

The home owner of this house and property is a millionaire.
Minimal damage to the house (living area) itself. Affected
the most, garage areas, as well as the backyards. The
next 8 photos are of the lower level of the damaged
house, as well as, the deck area in the backyard.

Beyond the deck is the Ocean (stairway
leads directly to the ocean waters).

This house is a summer rental, The house and its amenities
being rented for 6 weeks. The rental fee 6 thousand dollars
a week. Total of 36 thousand dollars. Paid in advance.

Photos show the old hardwood floors in
the processes of being remove.

The floors will be replaced.

Preparing to make an estimate regarding the amount
of the water damage that will be repaired.

Flooring that will be replaced after suffering water damage.

Water damage has ruined the door. Water damage existed inside of a house. The water level is recognized by the cut away section of sheet rock. Inside the room going beyond the door, mold is noticeable on the wall in between the shelves.

BEACH HAVEN

Water gets inside of the Beach Haven post office. Photos
illustrates the height of the water level, damaging the walls.

BEACH HAVEN-WEST

Outside the house appears to have escaped the wrath of Sandy.

Inside tells a different story. The interior is a shambles. The kitchen has water damage and mold appears under the table on the wall and furniture, where a jar of peanut butter sits.

SEASIDE HEIGHTS

The only vehicles allowed into Seaside Heights had to
display a contractors permit issued by the municipality.

National guardsmen stationed on the main thourofair to keep
non authorizedperson; i.e. non-residents, tourists, as well
as, residents that were evacuated from Seaside Heights.

Looking at a building totally destroyed by Sandy.

Photos show lots where buildings stood depicting
the rubble that is strewn all over the properties.

Lagoon: A shallow body of water being a channel, sound, or
pond near or communicating with a larger body of water.
An area of sea water that is seperated from the ocean.

Photos show lagoons battered and left in
disarray. Damage quite extensive.

Ducks appear not te be disturbed as a result of
the lagoons being wrecked by Sandy.

Warer damage required that this house be completely gutted.

Everything from the interior of this house being thrown away.

Residents belongings being thrown away.

The entire street effected by Sandy. Furnishings and appliances at
the curb of every house, which were lined up on the whole block.

Carpeting, furnishings, and appliances being discarded.

The top of this boat was sheared off, bottom portion
allegedly receives minimum or no damage.

Photos are only a fraction of the amount of discarded
appliances: stoves, air conditioners, washer and
dryers, chairs, tables, refrigerators and more.

Piles of house hold furnishings like this were
evident throughout the Jersey shore.

RESTORE THE
SHORE

Being displaced from Hurricane Sandy has been very difficult. Choosing and working with Westrum Homes to rebuild was easy! Their knowledge and timely responses to any questions via e-mail or phone has made the long road to recovery much easier for us. I recommend Westrum to our neighborsand friends who are still trying to move forward from the storm. Thank you Westrum Homes for coming to the Jersey Shore and helping us restore our beloved neighborhoods and beach towns!

Photos illustrates the use of pilings, that are in
place for the construction of a new house.

Pilings: A long slender (structure support) column comprised
of a length wood, steel, or other construction material
driven into the ground to support a vertical lead.

Photos are an example of a new house completed using
pilings, that are required to meet state guidelines.

New kitchen

Different look into the kitchen

New bedroom - without furnishings

Photos of a module being hoisted and placed on pilings.

Module: A set of standardized parts or independent units
that can be used to construct a more complex structure.
Example: Furniture or a building.

Module being constructed as a duplex.

RESTORE THE SHORE:

Asbury Park, Loch Arbor, Deal, Long Branch

Ship is called a dredge.
Dredge: An excavation activity usually carried out underwater.

Any of various powerful machines for removing

A piece of equipment that is used to strain
the sand going onto the beach.

The pipe is attached to the screen and is
going under water from the dredge.

Photos show the sand going onto the beach

The sand (silt), or the like carried by moving or
running water, and deposited onto the beach

Keeping the equipment in working order. Up keep
is very important to complete the job at hand.

Definition of Terms

Dredge - a machine or barge for removing earth or silt.

Silt - a fine earth: particles of such soil floating in rivers, ponds, or lakes; deposits (as by a river).

Wave base-height of a moving ridge or swell on the surface of water as the tide comes in or the tide goes out.

Pilings - a long slender column (wood or steel) driven into the grounds to support a vertical load.

Lagoon- a shallow sound, channel, or pond near or communicating with a larger body of water.

About the Author

Bronville Scott is originally from Jersey City, New Jersey. His family relocated when he was at an early age, moving to Neptune, New Jersey located in Monmouth County at the Jersey Shore. From 1968 until 1971, he served in the United States Army stationed at the Pentagon, Department of Defense, Washington, DC. After completing military service, he moved to California. While living in California, he secured a position as a newspaper reporter, columnist, and critic (reviewing stage plays, etc.). Returning to the East Coast, he had resided in the Oranges, Newark, New Jersey, and Monmouth County as well as Ocean County; he is presently residing in Toms River, N. J. with his wife, Priscilla Jordan - Scott. The married couple have two sons; Anthony and Jason.

On a dare, he submitted his poetry in a contest advertised in the Asbury Park Press, which was sponsored by Poetry.com. After submitting a couple of written works, the Poetry.com committee informed the author that any written poetry submitted by him will be automatically accepted by Poetry.com. His next project is to try to have the poetic lyrics set into music in the near future. By going into the website www.poetry.com and selecting the icon where it says Where's My Poem to search poems submitted before 2012, put in the name Bronville Scott and the title of six poems, submitted and accepted, will appear. He also is internationally published and received certificates as an outstanding poet through Poetry.com.

9 781683 486930